Inside the NFL

Washington Redskins

BY **RAMEY TEMPLE**

www.av2books.com

AV² provides enriched content that supplements and complements this book. Weigl's AV² books strive to create inspired learning and engage young minds in a total learning experience.

Your AV² Media Enhanced books come alive with...

 Audio
Listen to sections of the book read aloud.

 Key Words
Study vocabulary, and complete a matching word activity.

 Video
Watch informative video clips.

 Quizzes
Test your knowledge.

Go to **www.av2books.com,** and enter this book's unique code.

BOOK CODE

M 9 7 4 5 5 1

 Embedded Weblinks
Gain additional information for research.

 Slide Show
View images and captions, and prepare a presentation.

AV² by Weigl brings you media enhanced books that support active learning.

 Try This!
Complete activities and hands-on experiments.

... and much, much more!

Published by AV² by Weigl
350 5th Avenue, 59th Floor
New York, NY 10118
Websites: www.av2books.com   www.weigl.com

Library of Congress Control Number: 2014930785

ISBN 978-1-4896-0906-9 (hardcover)
ISBN 978-1-4896-0908-3 (single-user eBook)
ISBN 978-1-4896-0909-0 (multi-user eBook)

Printed in the United States of America in North Mankato, Minnesota
1 2 3 4 5 6 7 8 9 0 18 17 16 15 14

042014
WEP150314

Project Coordinator Aaron Carr
Art Director Terry Paulhus

Photo Credits
Every reasonable effort has been made to trace ownership and to obtain permission to reprint copyright material. The publishers would be pleased to have any errors or omissions brought to their attention so that they may be corrected in subsequent printings.

Weigl acknowledges Getty Images as its primary image supplier for this title.

Washington Redskins

CONTENTS

Introduction

The Washington Redskins are one of the oldest and most successful franchises in the National Football League (NFL). The team began winning immediately upon their arrival in Washington, D.C. in 1937. Over the next nine years, they would reach the championship game six times, winning in 1937 and 1942. Aside from nearly winning the **Super Bowl** in 1972, the Redskins then went through a period of losing, which peaked in 1961 when the team recorded a 1-12-1 win-loss-tie record.

Things changed right away with the hiring of Joe Gibbs in 1981. From there, a decade of winning took place that is nearly unmatched in NFL history.

Despite the overall success of the franchise, the Redskins last appeared in the Super Bowl in 1991.

Behind Doug Williams, Joe Theismann, John Riggins, Art Monk, and Darrell Green, the Redskins appeared in seven **postseasons**, captured four conference titles and won three Super Bowls. The Redskins hope to play in their sixth Super Bowl someday soon, with quarterback Robert Griffin III leading the way.

Robert Griffin III has been a quarterback for the Redskins since 2012.

REDSKINS

Stadium FedExField

Division National Football Conference (NFC) East

Head coach Jay Gruden

Location Landover, Maryland

Super Bowl titles 1982, 1987, 1991

Nicknames Skins

22
Playoff Appearances

3
Super Bowl Championships

11
Division Championships

PLACE OF HONOR

The Redskins have only retired one jersey number,

33

which was worn by Sammy Baugh from

1937 to 1952

 In Super Bowl XXII, Doug Williams became the first African American quarterback to win a championship.

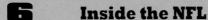

The Washington Redskins were founded by George Preston Marshall in 1932, and were known as the Boston Braves. They changed their name to the Redskins in 1933. Four years later, they moved to Washington, D.C. and found early success, winning championships in 1937 and 1942.

The next 30 years were filled with lots of losing. An exception was the 1972 season, when the Skins reached their first Super Bowl. In that game, they were stuffed by the Miami Dolphins. With Joe Gibbs at the helm a decade later, the Redskins got their revenge, beating the Fish 27-17 in Super Bowl XVII.

The Redskins found themselves back in the Super Bowl the following year, and lost. They were back again in 1987, when Doug Williams helped then win a second Vince Lombardi trophy. In 1991, it was Mark Rypien who helped the Redskins edge the Buffalo Bills in Super Bowl XXVI, for the Redskins' third championship in nine years.

In 1999, two years after moving to FedExField, investment banker Daniel Snyder bought the Redskins with the hope of getting them back to the Super Bowl. There have been ups and downs, but drafting Robert Griffin III and Alfred Morris in 2011 certainly has the Redskins on the right track.

Despite the numerous handoffs from Robert Griffin III to Alfred Morris, the two have only connected on 20 completions in their first 32 games together.

The Stadium

FedExField seats 79,000 fans, making it one of the largest stadiums in the NFL.

When the Redskins arrived in Washington in 1937, they played in Griffith Stadium, located in the heart of the city. Originally known as National Park, the steel and concrete structure was renamed for Washington Senators owner Clark Griffith in 1920. Griffith Stadium was home to the Redskins for more than

20 years. In 1961, the team moved to Robert F. Kennedy Memorial Stadium, the first major stadium to use a circular exterior design, which helped accommodate both baseball and football. Things got off to a rocky start at RFK. The Skins went 1-12-1, the worst season in team history.

In 1997, the Redskins left Washington and moved into the cavernous Jack Kent Cooke Stadium in suburban Maryland. The stadium was renamed FedExField in 1999 after new owner Daniel Snyder sold the naming rights. FedExField has five levels, each named after famous figures in Redskins history, as in George Preston Marshall Lower Level, Joe Gibbs Club Level, and Pete Rozelle Upper Level, to name a few.

 As of 2013, the Redskins and their dedicated fans had set single-season attendance records for nine straight years.

 Be sure to grab extra napkins before eating one of Ben's Famous All Meat Chili Dogs.

Where They Play

CANADA

Washington

Oregon

Montana

North Dakota

Minnesota

Lake Superior

Idaho

South Dakota

Wisconsin

Iowa

Illinois

30

23

22

24

13

Wyoming

Nevada

Utah

Colorado

Nebraska

Kansas

Missouri

29

15

14

31

California

UNITED STATES

16

Arizona

New Mexico

Oklahoma

Arkansas

32

Mississippi

Pacific Ocean

Texas

Louisiana

17

12

27

Alaska

Hawai'i

MEXICO

Gulf of Mexico

| 0 | 500 Miles |
| 0 | 500 km |

| 0 | 100 Miles |
| 0 | 100 km |

AMERICAN FOOTBALL CONFERENCE

EAST
1 Gillette Stadium
2 MetLife Stadium
3 Ralph Wilson Stadium
4 Sun Life Stadium

NORTH
5 FirstEnergy Stadium
6 Heinz Field
7 M&T Bank Stadium
8 Paul Brown Stadium

SOUTH
9 EverBank Field
10 LP Field
11 Lucas Oil Stadium
12 NRG Stadium

WEST
13 Arrowhead Stadium
14 Sports Authority Field at Mile High
15 O.co Coliseum
16 Qualcomm Stadium

FedExField

Location
1600 Fedex Way
Landover, Maryland

Broke ground
March 13, 1996

Completed
September 14, 1997

Surface
grass

Features
- high definition LED video displays that are 100 feet (30 meters) wide
- the end zone video boards can be split into multiple configurations, meaning more choices and information for fans

LEGEND
American Football Conference
National Football Conference
FedExField

Lake Michigan

Lake Huron

Lake Ontario

Lake Erie

New Hampshire

Vermont

Maine

Michigan

New York

Massachusetts

Rhode Island

Connecticut

Pennsylvania

New Jersey

Delaware

Maryland

Ohio

Indiana

West Virginia

Virginia

Kentucky

Tennessee

North Carolina

South Carolina

Georgia

Alabama

Atlantic Ocean

Florida

21 · 3 · 2 · 1 · 19 · 20 · 18 · 11 · 5 · 6 · 7 · 8 · 10 · 25 · 26 · 9 · 28 · 4

0 — 250 Miles
0 — 250 Kilometers

NATIONAL FOOTBALL CONFERENCE

EAST	NORTH	SOUTH	WEST
17 AT&T Stadium	21 Ford Field	25 Bank of America Stadium	29 Levi's Stadium
★ 18 FedExField	22 Lambeau Field	26 Georgia Dome	30 CenturyLink Field
19 Lincoln Financial Field	23 Mall of America Field	27 Mercedes-Benz Superdome	31 Edward Jones Dome
20 MetLife Stadium	24 Soldier Field	28 Raymond James Stadium	32 University of Phoenix Stadium

The Uniforms

SAFETY BEFORE STYLE

Until 2013, the Redskins' throwback uniform included an alternate helmet. A recent NFL rule no longer allows any team to use a secondary helmet, due to safety concerns.

In his first NFL season, Alfred Morris finished second in rushing yards.

Although Redskins uniforms have undergone plenty of changes over the years, the color scheme has remained white, burgundy, and gold. Their first uniforms consisted of gold pants with a burgundy jersey and a gold helmet. The **logo** on the sleeve was changed in 1952, but gold and burgundy continued to dominate.

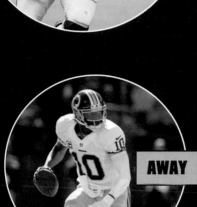

HOME

AWAY

The biggest changes took place in 1981, when coach Gibbs took over and the Redskins became one of three teams to wear white jerseys at home. The classic look, as it was known, was a white jersey and burgundy pants. The Skins have generally stuck with this look over the last 30 years.

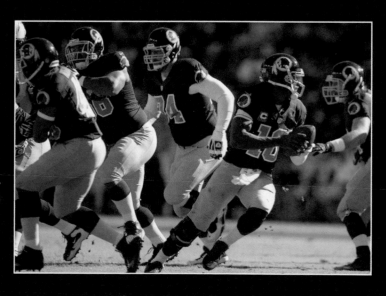

In celebration of the franchise's 75th anniversary, the Redskins wore a special throwback uniform for a 2007 home game versus the New York Giants.

The Helmets

HOME OR AWAY?

For many years, the Redskins were one of three teams that mainly wore their white jerseys at home. The other two were the Dallas Cowboys and Miami Dolphins.

Facemasks did not become mainstream in the NFL until 1962. Players did not start using full facemasks until 1975.

Beginning in 1937, the Redskins wore gold helmets. A red stripe appeared down the center of the helmet by 1951. Five years later in 1956, the main color on the helmet was burgundy, with a gold stripe highlighting it. The helmet remained burgundy, but a feather was added, right down the center of the helmet.

Inspired by coach Vince Lombardi and his recent success with the Green Bay Packers, the helmets turned yellow again in 1970. These helmets featured a red circle with a new logo, a simple "R," embedded on the side. The helmet made its last change in 1972, donning the Redskin logo that appears on the helmets today. Over the next 40 years, there were a few slight changes to the helmet, the most notable being the addition of the gold facemask in 1978.

In addition to helmets, leg and shoulder pads are required to keep players safe.

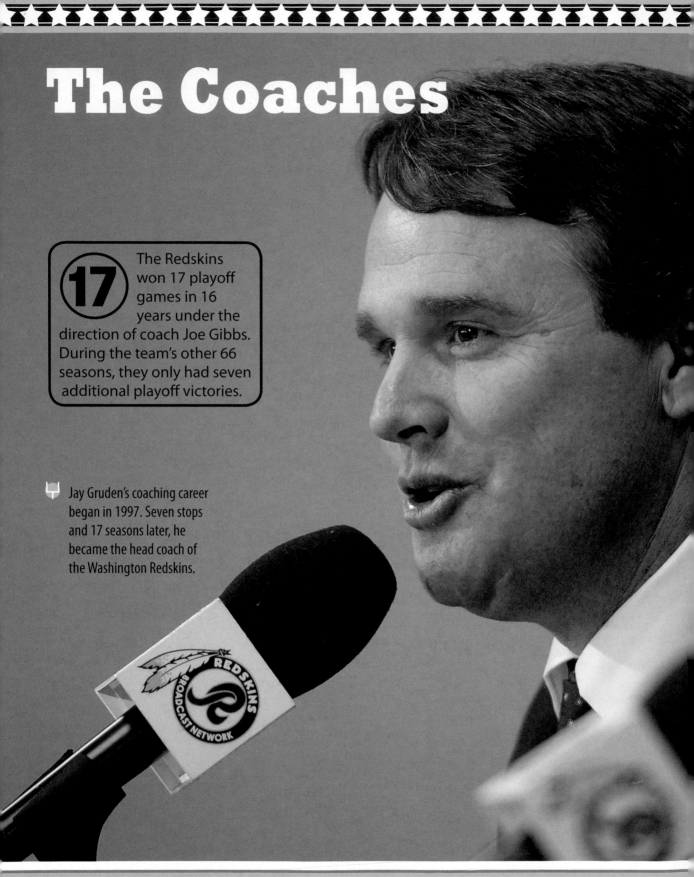

The Coaches

17 The Redskins won 17 playoff games in 16 years under the direction of coach Joe Gibbs. During the team's other 66 seasons, they only had seven additional playoff victories.

Jay Gruden's coaching career began in 1997. Seven stops and 17 seasons later, he became the head coach of the Washington Redskins.

The Washington Redskins have had 25 head coaches, with only seven of them having winning records. Ray Flaherty, George Allen, and Joe Gibbs are the most consistent winners, accounting for two NFL Championships, three Super Bowl victories, and five Super Bowl appearances. Since Daniel Synder bought the team in 1999, the Redskins have had eight different head coaches.

GEORGE ALLEN

Hall of famer George Allen led the Redskins to the **playoffs** in five of his seven seasons as coach, highlighted by a Super Bowl run in 1972. Allen may be most famous for taunting Dallas Cowboys players while wearing an Indian headdress, helping to build a great rivalry.

JOE GIBBS

Joe Gibbs is the winningest Redskins coach of all time, with 124 regular season wins and three Super Bowl victories. In 2004, Gibbs came out of retirement to rejoin the Redskins as head coach and team president. He was inducted into the Pro Football **Hall of Fame** in 1996.

JAY GRUDEN

Jay Gruden was hired by the Redskins just a few weeks after the 2013 regular season ended. Replacing a coach like Mike Shanahan is no easy task. A former quarterback, Gruden may be best equipped for the task of getting the most out of the young and talented Robert Griffin III.

Team Spirit

Despite the controversy surrounding the Redskins' name and logo, a 2013 USA Today poll indicated that 79 percent of Americans believed that the Redskins should keep their name.

Although the Redskins do not have an official mascot, the fans have picked up the slack with their spirit, selling out every home game since 1965. The unofficial mascot, Chief Zee, began attending home games in 1978, wearing a faux headdress, carrying a toy tomahawk, and leading the fans in cheers.

During the 1980s, another mascot developed. At the time, the Redskins were known for their powerful and gritty offensive line, which had been nicknamed the Hogs. In 1983, their success inspired a group of fans known as the Hoggettes. These 12 men attended home games wearing "old lady" dresses, wide-brimmed hats, and plastic pig snouts. The Hoggettes retired in 2013 after 30 years of displaying hilarious team spirit.

The Redskins' unofficial mascot, Chief Zee, had his tomahawk stolen at a 2008 home game. It was later returned.

 The "Hogs" nickname was originally given to the Redskins' superior offensive line during the 1980s and 1990s.

Legends of the Past

Many great players have suited up in the Redskins' burgundy and gold. A few of them have become icons of the team and the city it represents.

Darrell Green

Position Defensive Back
Seasons 20 (1983–2002)
Born February 15, 1960, in Houston, Texas

Playing 20 seasons for the same NFL team is a feat very few have accomplished. When he retired at 41, Darrell Green had played in 295 games, more than any defensive player in NFL history. The seven-time **Pro Bowler** was known for his ability to shut down opposing receivers by making up ground with his legendary speed. Green won the NFL's Fastest Man Competition a record four times and was considered the fastest man in the league for much of his playing career. The hall of famer had 54 interceptions in his career, grabbing at least one in 19 straight seasons, another NFL record.

Joe Theismann

Joe Theismann was a two-time Pro Bowler during 12 successful seasons with the Redskins. In addition to holding nearly every Redskins passing record, Theismann led the Skins to a victory over the Dolphins in Super Bowl XVII in 1982. This win marked their first championship in 40 years. His career was infamously cut short when New York Giants linebacker Lawrence Taylor **sacked** him during a Monday Night Football game in November of 1985, breaking his leg in a gruesome way. The Washington Post later referred to the incident as "The Hit That No One Who Saw It Can Ever Forget."

Position Quarterback
Seasons 12 (1974–1985)
Born September 9, 1949, in New Brunswick, New Jersey

Art Monk

The Redskins drafted hall of famer Art Monk in 1980, and began to win almost immediately. During his 14-year career, Monk helped capture three Super Bowl victories. Perhaps his greatest season was 1984, when he caught a then-NFL record 106 receptions for 1,372 yards. Monk was the first player in NFL history to record more than 102 receptions in a season and more than 900 receptions in a career. His NFL record for career receptions was broken by Jerry Rice in 1995, the last season Monk played.

Position Wide Receiver
Seasons 16 (1980–1995)
Born December 5, 1957, in White Plains, New York

John Riggins

John Riggins earned the nickname "The Diesel" by being big, strong, and tough. Riggins is a Super Bowl champion, a Super Bowl **Most Valuable Player (MVP)**, and a Hall of Famer. In 14 NFL seasons, he played 175 games, amassing 13,442 yards and 116 touchdowns. As great as he was in the regular season, it was the postseason where Riggins really distinguished himself, rushing 251 times for 996 yards and 12 touchdowns in nine post-season games. When "Riggo" scored his 100th career touchdown, he became the second player in NFL history to accomplish the feat, and the first since Jim Brown.

Position Running Back
Seasons 15 (1971–1985)
Born August 4, 1949, in Seneca, Kansas

Stars of Today

Today's Buccaneers team is made up of many young, talented players who have proven that they are among the best players in the league.

Alfred Morris

Alfred Morris was a sixth round pick in the 2012 **NFL Draft**, so it came as a bit of surprise when coach Shanahan announced that the rookie out of Florida Atlantic University would be his starting running back. Morris proved his coach right, rushing for 96 yards on 28 carries, while scoring two touchdowns. Morris did not look back. In fact, he became the fourth player in NFL history to record more than 1,600 rushing yards during his rookie season. Morris helped lead the Redskins to a division title in 2012, and hopes to anchor the **backfield** for years to come.

Position Running Back
Seasons 2 (2012–2013)
Born December 12, 1988, in Pensacola, Florida

Ryan Kerrigan

Ryan Kerrigan was an **All-American** at Purdue University, chosen in the first round of the 2011 NFL Draft by the Redskins. The speedy linebacker who seems to be everywhere on the field played in all 16 games during his rookie season. He recorded 63 tackles, had 7.5 sacks, forced four fumbles, had one interception, and even scored a touchdown. Kerrigan continued to work hard and improve the following season and was rewarded with a trip to the Pro Bowl. Although his strong play continued in 2013, the team had a down year.

Position Linebacker
Seasons 3 (2011–2013)
Born August 16, 1988, in Muncie, Indiana

Brian Orakpo

Playing All-American football at the University of Texas, while becoming known as one of the top defensive lineman in the country, Brian Orakpo was an easy choice for the Redskins at No. 13 overall in the 2009 draft. They were rewarded as Orakpo made it to the Pro Bowl in both of his first two NFL seasons. Although 2011 and 2012 were up-and-down seasons due to nagging injuries, Orakpo had perhaps his best season as a pro in 2013.

Position Linebacker
Seasons 5 (2009–2013)
Born July 31, 1986, in Houston, Texas

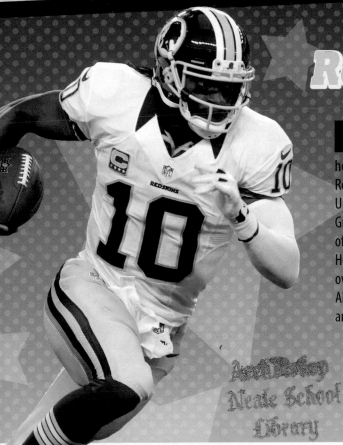

Robert Griffin III

Robert Griffin III, also known as RG3, won the **Heisman Trophy** in 2011, quickly becoming the hottest player in the country not named Andrew Luck. The Redskins traded up for the rights to draft the electric Baylor University quarterback second overall in the 2012 NFL Draft. Griffin was named the starter from day one and tossed a pair of touchdowns while throwing for 320 yards in his first game. He went on to help the Skins capture their first division title in over a decade while winning NFL Offensive Rookie of the Year. Although an injured knee slowed him in 2013, the Redskins are thrilled to have Griffin as their quarterback of the future.

Position Quarterback
Seasons 2 (2012–2013)
Born February 12, 1990, in Okinawa Prefecture, Japan

All-Time Records

91 **All Time Sacks** Defensive end Dexter Manley got to the quarterback almost 100 times during his nine years in the trenches for the Redskins.

1,613 **Single-Season Rushing Yards**

In 2012, a sixth round draft pick named Alfred Morris came out of nowhere to win the Redskins starting running back job. Morris carried the ball 335 times in setting a new Skins rushing record.

4,109

Single Season Passing Yards

The single-season record for passing yards does not belong to Sammy Baugh, or Joe Theismann. In 1986, it was Jay Schroeder who became the first Redskin quarterback to break the 4,000-yard mark.

7,472 All-time Rushing Yards

In 1983, John Riggins rushed for a career-best 1,347 yards and scored 24 touchdowns, a year after winning Super Bowl MVP. He is the Skins all-time leader in rushing yards and rushing touchdowns.

12,026 All-time Receiving Yards

Art Monk accumulated more than 1,000 receiving yards in five of the 14 seasons he spent with the Redskins.

Timeline

Throughout the team's history, the Washington Redskins have had many memorable events that have become defining moments for the team and its fans.

1982
Kicker Mark Moseley leads the Redskins during a strike-shortened season, winning the NFL MVP award. The Redskins cruise through the playoffs and win the Super Bowl 27-17 over the Miami Dolphins. Riggins earns the Super Bowl MVP.

1937
After playing in Boston since 1932, the Redskins made their Washington debut, beating the Giants 13-3 at Griffith Stadium.

In 1985, a national audience watches in horror as Theismann is hit by several New York Giant defenders, ending his career in gruesome fashion.

| 1935 | 1945 | 1955 | 1965 | 1975 | 1985 |

1942
With a record of 10-1, the Redskins win the East and beat the Chicago Bears to win the NFL Championship.

1962
The Redskins finally integrate their roster, becoming the last team to do so. They trade their top draft pick to the Cleveland Browns for wide receiver Bobby Mitchell, who goes on to have a huge season.

1983
The Redskins go 14-2, marking their best regular season finish in franchise history. Defending a Super Bowl title proves difficult against the Los Angeles Raiders, as they get the best of Theismann in a 38-9 blowout in Super Bowl XVIII.

1972
Running back Larry Brown wins the NFL MVP award by scoring 12 touchdowns and collecting 1,689 **all-purpose yards**. The Redskins host the Green Bay Packers and then the Dallas Cowboys on their way to Super Bowl VII, but fall to the Dolphins 14-7. The Fish finish 17-0 on the year, recording the only perfect season in NFL history.

1987

Doug Williams emerges from a quarterback controversy and leads the Redskins through the playoffs, landing them back in the big game for the third time in six years. The Skins blast the Denver Broncos 42-10 in Super Bowl XXII as Doug Williams becomes the first African-American quarterback to start and win a Super Bowl.

The Future

The Redskins had two of the top five choices for NFL Offensive Player of the Year in 2012 and both were rookies. Needless to say that the future is bright for the Skins behind their electric quarterback RG3, and their dynamic young running back, Alfred Morris. The last time the Redskins were this loaded with talented young players they built a 10-year **dynasty** and captured three Super Bowl championships. They hope this group is next.

After the 2009 season, Synder hires two-time Super Bowl winning coach, Mike Shanahan.

1990 1995 2000 2005 2010 2015

In 1991, quarterback Mark Rypien earns Super Bowl MVP honors as the Skins beat the Bills 37-24 in Super Bowl XXVI in Minneapolis.

2012

The Robert Griffin III era starts with a bang, as the Redskins rookie quarterback leads the Redskins to a 40-32 week one win against the New Orleans Saints. Griffin becomes the first quarterback to pass for more than 300 yards in his first NFL game. The Redskins go on to win the NFC East, and RG3 earns NFL Offensive Player of the Year.

1999

The Cooke family is forced to sell the team. The buyer is Daniel Snyder, a New York investment banker. Snyder immediately sells the stadium naming rights and Jack Kent Cooke Stadium becomes FedExField.

Write a Biography

Life Story

A person's life story can be the subject of a book. This kind of book is called a biography. Biographies often describe the lives of people who have achieved great success. These people may be alive today, or they may have lived many years ago. Reading a biography can help you learn more about a great person.

Get the Facts

Use this book, and research in the library and on the Internet, to find out more about your favorite Redskin. Learn as much about this player as you can. What position does he play? What are his statistics in important categories? Has he set any records? Also, be sure to write down key events in the person's life. What was his childhood like? What has he accomplished off the field? Is there anything else that makes this person special or unusual?

Use the Concept Web

A concept web is a useful research tool. Read the questions in the concept web on the following page. Answer the questions in your notebook. Your answers will help you write a biography.

Concept Web

Adulthood
- Where does this individual currently reside?
- Does he or she have a family?

Your Opinion
- What did you learn from the books you read in your research?
- Would you suggest these books to others?
- Was anything missing from these books?

Childhood
- Where and when was this person born?
- Describe his or her parents, siblings, and friends.
- Did this person grow up in unusual circumstances?

Accomplishments off the Field
- What is this person's life's work?
- Has he or she received awards or recognition for accomplishments?
- How have this person's accomplishments served others?

Write a Biography

Help and Obstacles
- Did this individual have a positive attitude?
- Did he or she receive help from others?
- Did this person have a mentor?
- Did this person face any hardships?
- If so, how were the hardships overcome?

Accomplishments on the Field
- What records does this person hold?
- What key games and plays have defined his or her career?
- What are his or her stats in categories important to his or her position?

Work and Preparation
- What was this person's education?
- What was his or her work experience?
- How does this person work; what is the process he or she uses?

Trivia Time

Take this quiz to test your knowledge of the Washington Redskins.
The answers are printed upside-down under each question.

1 What was the name of the stadium the Redskins began playing in during the 1937 season?

A. Griffith Stadium

2 In what year did the Redskins win their first NFL Championship?

A. 1937

3 Whose tomahawk was stolen at a Redskins home game?

A. Chief Zee

4

A. three (1982, 1987, 1991)

5 Who are the three Super Bowl winning quarterbacks in Redskins history?

A. Joe Theismann, Doug Williams, and Mark Rypien

6 What position did Art Monk play?

A. Wide Receiver

7 Which Redskins player won the NFL's Fastest Man Competition a record four times?

A. Darrell Green

8 In what city and state is FedExField located?

A. Landover, Maryland

9 What year did Daniel Snyder buy the Redskins?

A. 1999

10 What other name does Robert Griffin III go by?

A. RG3

Key Words

All-American: a player, usually in high school or college, judged to be the best in each position of a sport

all-purpose yards: also referred to as combined net yards, all-purpose yards are a statistic that measures total yardage gained on receptions, runs from scrimmage, punt returns, and kickoff returns

backfield: the area of play behind either the offensive or defensive line

dynasty: a team that wins a series of championships in a short period of time

hall of fame: a group of persons judged to be outstanding in a particular sport

Heisman Trophy: an annual award given to the college football player who best demonstrates excellence and hard work

logo: a symbol that stands for a team or organization

most valuable player (MVP): the player judged to be most valuable to his team's success

NFL Draft: an annual event where the NFL chooses college football players to be new team members

playoffs: the games played following the end of the regular season. Six teams are qualified: the four winners of the different conferences, and the two best teams that did not finish first in their respective conference, the wild cards

postseasons: sporting events that takes place after the end of the regular season

Pro Bowler: NFL players who take part in the annual all-star game that pits the best players in the National Football Conference against the best players in the American Football Conference

sacked: a sack occurs when the quarterback is tackled behind the line of scrimmage before he can throw a forward pass

Super Bowl: the NFL's annual championship game between the winning team from the NFC and the winning team from the AFC

Index

Log on to www.av2books.com

AV² by Weigl brings you media enhanced books that support active learning. Go to www.av2books.com, and enter the special code found on page 2 of this book. You will gain access to enriched and enhanced content that supplements and complements this book. Content includes video, audio, weblinks, quizzes, a slide show, and activities.

AV² Online Navigation

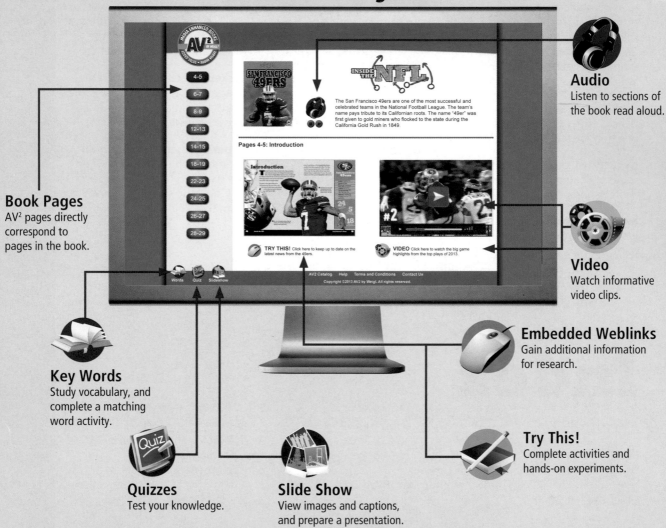

Book Pages
AV² pages directly correspond to pages in the book.

Key Words
Study vocabulary, and complete a matching word activity.

Quizzes
Test your knowledge.

Slide Show
View images and captions, and prepare a presentation.

Audio
Listen to sections of the book read aloud.

Video
Watch informative video clips.

Embedded Weblinks
Gain additional information for research.

Try This!
Complete activities and hands-on experiments.

AV² was built to bridge the gap between print and digital. We encourage you to tell us what you like and what you want to see in the future.

Sign up to be an AV² Ambassador at www.av2books.com/ambassador.